I0834819

The Manger on The Mantle

A Christmas Tale
Based on *Two* True Stories

Other Books by Bill Wylson

Hieroglyphs, Golden Plates & Typos

Give Place in Your Heart

Three Minutes Eighteen Seconds

Elder Hammond and The Inspector

Available at:

myldsbooks.com
greenstempress.com

The Manger on The Mantle

A Christmas Tale
Based on *Two* True Stories

By BILL WYLSON

Green Stem Press

ISBN-13: 978-1-7342387-0-9
ISBN-10: 1-7342387-0-4

Green Stem Press
A White Horse Book

Printed in the U.S.A.

greenstempress.com
myldsbooks.com

"If your life
Is a leaf
That the seasons
Tear off and condemn,

He will bind you with love
That is graceful
And green as a stem."

Leonard Cohen – *paraphrased*

Table of Contents

ACKNOWLEDGMENTS:

I gratefully acknowledge the teachings that my mother and father have indelibly engraved onto my heart and echo the words of Enos; "praised be the name of my God for it."

And

I thank my beautiful wife, Connie, whose gospel light shines so brightly that it reaches even into the darkest corners of my heart.

DISCLAIMER:

I never quite understood why we say that 'names have been changed to protect the innocent'. I think what we mean is that the names have been changed to protect the innocent author from libel lawsuits. So, although this story is based on actual events, the names, including the name of the horse, have all been changed to protect the innocent (as well as the not so innocent.)

No horses were harmed in the writing of this book.

DEDICATION:

To my childhood friend,
Johnny Morrison
who passed away too soon at age 34.

Chapter One

Earth to Mars

I'd like to paint you a picture.

It's the picture of an idyllic American childhood.

I'd like to tell you the story of an all-American boy who grew up to become a successful businessman; a loving and devoted husband; a gentle, kind and caring father and a deeply religious and contributing member of society. But that story would be a lie.

Because this is *my* story.

My name is Mark Spencer and I was born in Hilliard, Ohio. Hilliard in the wintertime is as picturesque as any Norman Rockwell painting. The forest behind my childhood home, lush and green in summer, now stands stark and bare and wrapped in a covering of gray sky. On an ordinary afternoon, as the silent snow settles gently to the forest floor, you could almost imagine Robert Frost stopping by with his horse to watch the 'woods fill up with snow.'

But this is not an ordinary afternoon, it is the day before Christmas and the silence of the woods with its drifting downy flakes is disturbed by the loud yet delightful laughter of little children, myself included, gathered in a forest clearing, occupied in an invigorating game of *Duck, Duck, Goose.* Dressed in winter coats and galoshes, wrapped in knitted scarves with matching mittens and wearing whatever Gosh-awful hats our mothers had forced onto our little heads, we ran in circles through the snow.

To this small child, Hilliard was the entire world, stretching infinitely through space and time; vast, peaceful and permanent. It was a paradise as hallowed and as innocent as any Eden.

Summers were spent climbing giant Mulberry trees and gorging ourselves on the delicious little fruit until our tummies ached; running through infinite fields of towering corn; swinging off ropes that hung from trees above the creek; skinning knees and scraping elbows. It was a time of racing my big sister, Linda, to *Lawson's Five and Dime* to waste my weekly allowance on plastic toy army men or the latest life-like *Creature from the Black Lagoon,* while Linda poured through packs of *Beatles* bubble gum cards, her heart set on finding another gorgeous picture of George Harrison to press devotedly between the pages of her diary.

In Winter we ice skated on the pond down by the cemetery and sledded on sloping landscapes wherever we could find them. We built igloos and snow forts and battled with other children from the neighborhood in intense snowball combat. And life was good.

We knew nothing of politics or impeachment, nothing of the draft or Vietnam, and war was just a game we played in the park after school. The little town of Hilliard with its farms and fairgrounds, its forests and streams, its peaceful Americana atmosphere was our vast, entire world. And time, to me at least, seemed interminable.

The only knowledge I had of a world outside of Hilliard was garnered from the peaceful Sunday mornings when mother and father would pack their five kids into the old '57 Chevy and drive us across the Scioto River into that sprawling metropolis, the capital city of Columbus, Ohio, for church services.

It was a more innocent time back then and I, well, … I was a more innocent person.

As the afternoon skies darkened and the clouds weighed heavy, the game of *Duck, Duck, Goose* grew wearisome and tedious. Kevin Mars, a bit of a neighborhood bully but fortunately, for me at least, my best friend at the time, decided to liven things up by throwing a snowball at my little sister, Cheryl. It hit her square in the face. Frantic children leapt to their feet and scattered for the safety of the trees, grabbing a handful of snow as they did to return fire on Kevin or whomever was still out in the open.

The snowball that hit Cheryl must have contained a small rock or sharp piece of ice because it left a small cut beneath my little sister's left eye. She sat in the snow silently sobbing, remnants of the spent weapon still pressed against her soft, rosy cheeks. Undaunted by the onslaught of snowballs, my older brother, Rick, a long and lanky awkward kid who deftly resembled Mike Nesmith of the *Monkees* in every way, including the wool beanie he wore on his head, slogged through the snow toward Kevin, shoving him face down on the frozen ground.

"Watch what you're doing, punk!" my brother hollered.

Kevin scampered to his feet like a frightened little squirrel and ran off into the woods. Bully or not, he was no match for my big brother. Rick lifted Cheryl onto his shoulders, and we headed toward home, arriving cold and wet but extremely animated. Even little Cheryl had forgotten her insignificant and trivial scrape as thoughts of Christmas returned.

Brightly colored lights adorned the eaves of our modest home and flickering electric candles burned in the picture window. From the sidewalk in front of the house we could see the partially decorated Christmas tree, centered in front of the living room window and towering upward until it practically touched our ceiling.

Earlier in the week, father had driven us to a Christmas tree lot on the outskirts of town to locate the perfect tree. All of us kids were allowed to choose our favorite tree, (well, all except Jennifer, the youngest, who had been appropriately nicknamed Jenny-poo,) father then selected the best of the four to place in our home. And just like the year before, and the year before that, it was my brother Rick's tree that dad had preferred.

As we entered the living room after our romp in the woods, we could see the presents wrapped in bright colored paper and tied with intricate ribbons and bows spread across the floor beneath the tree's emerald boughs. These were just the gifts that we gave to each other. The real treat would be the presents that Santa Claus brought once we were all asleep.

Over dinner that evening, father noticed the cut on Cheryl's cheek.

"What happened to you, Sweetie?"

Suddenly, this little girl who had seemingly recovered from her minor scrape over two hours ago began to quiver. Her bottom lip trembled, and her bright blue eyes glazed over with tiny tears.

"That stupid Kevin, he threw a snowball and it, and it hit me…" and now the dam burst, and the tears flowed freely, "… it hit me right in my face. Right there, daddy," she wailed, pointing at the tiny scratch on her cheek.

"Well, we'll just have to do something about that," my father announced. Standing up from his chair at the head of the table, he stepped toward the phone that hung on the kitchen wall.

"It wasn't anything, dad," I protested, trying to defend my friend. "Kevin didn't mean to hurt her."

"I know, son."

I wasn't a popular kid on the playground but Kevin, although he was a bully, took a liking to me. At recess, he would get me in a headlock and then parade me around the playground making me 'moo' at the other children.

"Whada'ya think of my pet cow?" he'd ask, and the kids all laughed, especially the girls.

It wasn't the best of friendships by any means, but it was better than feeling alone and left out and I didn't want it messed with by an excessively meddlesome father.

Of course, all of us at the table that night, well, all but baby Jennifer, knew the real reason dad was calling Kevin's father and it had nothing to do with Cheryl's insignificant scrape.

As dad dialed the phone, we waited for it. It was an inevitable agony as constant and as certain as the rising sun.

"Mars residence," the voice on the other end of the phone announced.

"Mars! This is Earth speaking."

It never failed. To this day I cannot imagine how annoying it must have been for Kevin's father whenever my dad telephoned him. I buried my head in my hands out of sheer embarrassment. Dad casually told Kevin's father that his son should be more careful about throwing snowballs and the conversation ended with my father silently savoring his superlative sense of humor.

Our Christmas Eve was traditionally spent stringing popcorn and cranberries, while father put the finishing touches of lights and tinsel on the tree and mother arranged the manger scene on the mantle place. Our mother and father both attempted to make Jesus Christ the center of our Christmas traditions and celebrations but the tiny manger was grossly overpowered by the splendidly decorated evergreen, the plentiful gifts and the bright red stockings that hung from the mantle directly below the lowly manger.

I remember how mother always placed the porcelain manger with its brightly painted yellow star in the center of the mantle. Inside the manger she would then place the donkey and two little lambs, and the cow that lay resting in the corner. An adoring Mary knelt inside the manger with Joseph standing tall and proud at her side. Just outside the little manger stood two shepherds leaning in and holding their crocks close to their sides. Two of the wise men stood upright, the third knelt near the opening of the manger, his arms extended, offering his gift of frankincense to the baby King.

I never knew if it was deliberate or not, but mother always waited until the last to place the tiny trough, filled with painted yellow hay and holding baby Jesus, the Son of God, in the center of the little manger scene. Before bed, father would gather us around the fireplace and read to us the entire second chapter of Luke. We listened, somewhat attentively, but mostly with our eyes on the presents beneath the tree as he read:

> "And it came to pass in those days, that there went out a decree from Cæsar Augustus, that all the world should be taxed….
>
> "… And Joseph also went up from Galilee, out of the city of Nazareth, into Judæa, unto the city of David, which is called Bethlehem; (because he was of the house and lineage of David:)
>
> "To be taxed with Mary his espoused wife, being great with child.
>
> "And she brought forth her firstborn son, and wrapped him in swaddling clothes, and laid him in a manger; because there was no room for them in the inn."

After the scripture reading, we knelt in a close

circle in the middle of the living room for family prayers. This was not just a Christmas tradition. Every evening our father marshaled us together to thank our Savior for daily blessings and to ask for needed help and guidance.

After the prayer, and after homemade cookies and a glass of milk were set out for Santa, the children were allowed to open one present before we were shuffled off to bed so that bikes could be put together, dollhouses set up, batteries installed and for whatever other 'some assembly required' items demanded parental attention before sun up.

Despite my parents' sincere effort to keep Christ in our hearts and minds, especially at this time of year, the commercialism of Christmas that surrounded the town, filled the shop windows, occupied store catalogs and spewed incessantly from our old black-and-white television set, engaged our attention more than anything else. We understood that this little manger and the birth of Jesus were the reason we celebrated this singular holiday, but to a child such as me, Santa was the real hero of this season.

And for some reason, on this particular Christmas, at least, those wondrous visions of sugarplums did not come dancing easily into my head.

Chapter Two

The Longest Night

Sleep completely eluded me as I imagined the fun I would have once Christmas morning finally arrived. I tossed and turned in my little bed. I wondered all night what terrific toy was waiting for me under the tree. I had asked for a Tonka back-hoe. I also wanted the new G. I. Joe Desert Trooper.

I secretly hoped for a sleek Stingray bicycle with gorilla handlebars and a banana seat, but I didn't truly expect to get one. When I had explained to my father how I absolutely needed a Stingray, because, well, *all* the kids in the neighborhood had one, he casually expounded the dynamics of the gear-to-wheel ratio of a bicycle with undersized tires like the Stingray and educated me on how I would have to petal twice as much to go a similar distance as I would on my old, beat-up and boyishly abused Schwinn Speedster. I sensed that the coveted Stingray would not be under the tree this year.

The same thing had happened the year before when I had insisted on a new drum set. I had dreamed of becoming the next Ginger Baker or John Bonham, but father explained to me that 95% of all musicians never earn a living at their craft no matter how proficiently they played. It was simply a matter of mathematics and statistics that had robbed me of my desired dreams.

Still, hope springs eternal, they say, and I simply could not stop thinking about the prestige I would garner riding my brand-new bicycle through town.

"Rick," I called softly to my brother sleeping in the upper bunk above me.

No answer.

"Hey, Rick," I repeated a little louder.

"Whaaat?" came the annoyed response.

"What time is it, Rick?"

From the vantage point of the upper bunk my brother could see the clock that hung on our bedroom wall. I couldn't.

"It's ten after six," he sleepily answered.

"Ten after six?" I enthusiastically sat up in bed. "Shouldn't we be getting up, then?"

"I dunno. Go ask dad."

I couldn't understand it. Why wasn't he as excited as I was? Why weren't my sisters clamoring down the stairs to see what Santa had brought them? Was I the only one anxious to open presents?

I determined to venture into the 'No Kids Zone' also known as my parents' bedroom. If it really is ten after six, we should all be getting up anyway. Someone had really dropped the ball on this one—big time!

Mom and dad were fast asleep as I approached the side of the bed that my father slept on.

"Hey, dad," I said quietly.

Only the sound of gentle snoring in the dark returned. I lightly shook my old man's arm.

"Dad. Hey, dad, can we get up now?" I asked.

He stirred. He reached for his eyeglasses and, slipping them on, picked up the wristwatch he always placed on the nightstand beside his bed.

"For crying out loud, it's two-thirty in the morning," came his perturbed response. "Go back to bed!"

The glasses dropped to the nightstand as my father's head returned to the soft recesses of his pillow. Why had my brother told me it was ten after six if it's only two-thirty? I climbed back into bed. Was this night ever going to end? I continued to toss, and I continued to turn, and sleep remained as elusive as the proverbial butterfly. The minutes dripped like thick molasses from a maple tree in winter.

I couldn't stand it any longer. I had to know what Santa had brought. I climbed from my bed and gathered all the courage I could muster. I would again venture into my parents' room. It had to be Christmas morning by now.

I tip-toed around the large bed. Soft snoring stirred the silence.

"Wait a minute," I thought to myself. "Is that mom? Nah, couldn't be. Girls don't snore."

At my father's bedside once again, I picked up and peered at his wristwatch. Four a.m., I think. Had it only been an hour and a half? I couldn't believe it, but I wouldn't risk waking my dad a second time. That would spell disaster. So, I quietly left their room and I lied down in the hallway in front of the living room.

From where I lay, I could see the Christmas tree, it's colored lights shining in the dark living room, illuminating presents that had not been there before. Santa had come! There was no Stingray bike but there were tons of other cool stuff, all wrapped and waiting for morning to make its much-anticipated appearance. As I wondered what new treasures now lay beneath the tree, my eyes rested on the little manger on the mantle, lit only by the lights on our Christmas tree, and I drifted off into a deep and peaceful sleep.

Chapter Three

Christmas in L.A.

"I think it's wrong, disgusting and obscene," I adamantly announced to my best friend, Johnny, as we drove toward the cliffs of Palos Verdes.

"What's wrong and disgusting?"

Johnny, a native Los Angelino who loves the warm air, the sandy beaches, earthquakes (apparently), and even palm trees decorated with blinking Christmas lights, knew exactly what I was talking about.

"Christmas without snow, Santas on surfboards and, yes, Christmas lights on palm trees. Ya' might as well be celebrating Christmas in July. There's no sleigh bells, no winter wonderland, no roasting chestnuts or drinking hot chocolate by a warm, roaring fire. It's wrong and it's just plain disgusting."

"I can get ya' a hot cocoa if you like," Johnny offered. "And *nobody* roasts chestnuts any more anyway. I mean, do you even know what a chestnut is?"

"You're missing the point," I replied.

"Look at it this way," Johnny responded. "If it weren't warm and pleasant out, if this gorgeous sun weren't shining down on us right now and we were knee deep in slushy snow freezing our butts off, shoveling our driveways and slipping on ice, we wouldn't be heading up to the stable to spend the afternoon horseback riding."

"Point taken," I said. "But I haven't been up to see Kohana in weeks."

Kohana, a Sioux word meaning swift, is my horse. She's a beautiful Pinto that stands fifteen and a half hands tall. Horseback riding was a love I had acquired when I was still a kid living in Hilliard and I hated the thought of not riding, and though Los Angeles is a far stretch from the open farmland of Ohio, I could still ride the trails and along the cliffs of the Palos Verdes peninsula.

"So what?" Johnny questioned.

"So Kohana's stall is going to be a nightmare. She hasn't been moved in two weeks," I replied. "You're gonna spend the afternoon riding. I'm going to spend it cleaning out her stall. Honestly, I'd rather be shoveling snow!"

Growing up I discovered that time is relative. As a small child I had believed that the life I knew would never end and my simple world of wonders and splendor would remain forever; and yet, a quarter of a century had come and gone in the blink of an eye and I ascertained that there actually was a world beyond the confines of cornfields, county fairs and country Christmases. There was a Disneyland and a Hollywood and the Wiltern Theater and poets and writers and artists who secluded themselves in places like Laurel Canyon. And there was status and power and prestige. And there was money to be made; lots of money and lots of ways to make it.

And maybe, maybe there was still child-like innocence somewhere in the world, but not in mine.

After graduating from Ohio State, I secured a job as a commercial copywriter for the Andrews Advertising Agency in southern California. I moved to Redondo Beach and biked the strand each day (though not on a Stingray) to my high-rise office in Marina Del Rey.

I was fascinated by the advertising business. Even as a teenager I was more interested in television commercials than I was in the Sitcoms they sponsored. Something about the power of persuasion captivated me. Perhaps it began from seeing my mom shed a tear whenever she read one of the corny poems I had written for her.

The thought that I could inspire an emotion, or even an action, made the advertising industry extremely appealing to me. If I could make someone spend their hard-earned wages on something they didn't want, they didn't need, they would probably never use but somehow felt that they couldn't live without, that felt like power to me. It felt like, well, it felt like getting someone in a headlock and making them moo.

My first ad campaign with Andrew's Advertising was for Poga Cookies, a European cookie brand that wanted to expand to America. I created a Sigmund Freud-type character whose patients had become "poga-noid" after tasting these delectable delights. Instead of curing his clients, Freud himself becomes "poga-noid" just listening to their detailed descriptions of the delicious cookies. The ads were a hit and I was on my way to a successful career.

I was introduced to Johnny by a friend from work. He was a songwriter who had a band that was struggling to be discovered. After reading some of my poetry, he asked me to write lyrics for him. I imagined us as the next Elton and Bernie song writing team.

We were soon working 2 a.m. recording sessions and putting on shows at Disneyland, and in Las Vegas and Reno. We even performed at places like the Blah Blah Café, a punk rock dive in downtown L. A., because the band's manager was just Johnny's dad, a used car salesman from Alameda.

Eventually, I married a surfer girl from Santa Monica whom I met during a band performance in Reno. We had a couple of kids and life, on the surface at least, seemed complete. Late nights at the office followed by later nights at the recording studios in Culver City began to take its toll, however, and the sordid life that lay beneath the surface began to show.

I knew only one way to raise a family and that was the way my father had raised me. I tried to do the same, to be as good a man, as good a husband, and as good a father as he had been. But I wasn't that man and it only contributed to my downfall. I tried too hard. I attempted to force ideals and values and a lifestyle that even I couldn't live up to, on my little family. As I tried to influence my family down a strait and narrow road, I was wandering down any dark side street that presented itself.

After a few years my wife had had enough of feeling inadequate and underrated and she ran off with a paramedic from Palm Springs. I guess it would have taken a paramedic to get her heart going again. And that was when my idyllic little world began to spiral out of control at an ever-increasing speed.

One thing I was right about: The stall was a nightmare. The manure and muck and defecation Kohana had created and trampled into the hay and mud was about a foot deep in her tiny stall.

The Palos Verdes peninsula where I stabled Kohana is located just south of Los Angeles. Rancho Palos Verdes, a suburb of Los Angeles, is known for its overpriced homes situated amidst large tracts of open land with unrestrained views of the Pacific Ocean. This is where the wanna-be wealthy hang out, the ones who can't afford Beverly Hills or Bel Air but still consider themselves too snooty to dwell with the common riffraff in the valley below. The unencumbered hills and the cliffs with their far-reaching vistas of ocean and Santa Catalina Island, make this an ideal location for horseback riding.

But renting a stable in Palos Verdes is not an inexpensive undertaking and consequently, I had to take one of the smaller stalls for my enormous horse. Working as much as I did while attempting to raise two small children as a single parent, left me little time to care for an extremely neglected animal. So, while Johnny took Kohana out for a much-needed gallop among the hills, I donned a pair of knee-high galoshes, grabbed a rake and shovel, and began the unholy task of cleaning up after my horse.

The stables were built in a high, wooded area with several winding trails. The area was not as dense as the forests of my childhood, but it reminded me of home. A warm wind blew off the ocean while the stench of the stall assaulted my nostrils. Sweat dripped from my forehead. Every step I took inside the steel railing sank me about six inches deep in muck. Kohana's stall was more like the bottom of an outhouse than a comfortable place to park a mare.

I labored for several hours that afternoon, lifting heavy shovel loads of the wet and messy manure into a rusty old wheelbarrow. Filling the wheelbarrow, I'd push my precious cargo to a nearby sloping hill and dump it down the side. With Christmas just three days away, I felt like the elf in charge of the renowned reindeers' barn.

I was glad Johnny had come along, not to help with the cleaning, but to give Kohana some exercise and her coveted run through the woods. By the time he returned from his ride along the cliffs, I had almost finished but I was too tired to ride. Bidding my horse good-bye, I headed back home.

Chapter Four

Root Beer Floats

The kids had gone with their mom for the holidays and I was looking forward to a quiet evening at home. After a shower and a light supper, I sat down in front of the television to relax for a while. When I wasn't working, riding or with my kids, television was my only escape. And I needed an escape, a place to hide out, a way to not deal with my emotions.

I despised the stigma of being divorced. My heart filled with anger and hatred and revenge. I wanted to hurt the people who had hurt me, in fact, I wanted to hurt anyone I could. And I did. I hurt my children who were the innocent victims of adult problems and sickness. I hurt my parents and tried to blame my father for the wrongs that I had done in life. Like the man at the stable stepping into the mire and the muck, I sunk deeper into depravity all the while pretending to be an adoring father, a successful businessman and a worthy member of my church and society.

What added to my personal misery was the fact that my ex-wife's parents attended the same church that I did. During the week I kept myself busy with work and with my two children as I struggled to deal with my disintegrating life, and I managed. Just barely perhaps but I managed. Sundays were another story. Where I went to be spiritually uplifted, I ended up being thrown deeper into depression and despair. Not only was it painful seeing my ex-in-laws, but half the congregation had sided with my ex- and I didn't know what friendships I had left or what support remained for me there.

Johnny suggested that I stop going to church if it bothered me so intensely, but I couldn't. Church was the last spiritual lifeline I held. Sure, I was living a depraved life, I was going against the Christian values I had been brought up with, living the life of a hypocrite at best, but if I gave up church, if I let go of that final lifeline, I knew I could be lost forever.

The steeper I fell into guilt, the harder I tried to promote the façade I had been living behind. I was, after all, in the advertising business, and I could sell ice cubes to Eskimos if I had to. So, I served actively in my church and I volunteered in the community, reading to the blind and working with the handicapped. I both fought and coddled the monster I had become at the same time. I felt that my soul had turned empty and hollow.

There was no doubt about it, the Spirit of God had withdrawn from my life. Sure, Seinfeld and the Simpsons could provide a few good laughs and a distraction, but I needed more than a laugh; I needed saving.

On an intellectual level, I understood that God loves the sinner though He hates the sin, but I felt no love in my life. I had grown distant from any spiritual feeling or moral commitment that I had ever experienced growing up. In essence, I was lost. Very, very lost.

As I settled down for the evening a knock came at the door and an expletive quietly slipped through my lips.

"Who the…," I began to say to myself and then I remembered.

"Marvin," I mumbled under my breath.

One Saturday evening, the week my divorce had finalized, a particularly miserable week by-the-way, a similar knock had come to my door. Reluctantly, I opened it that day to find Marvin, an older member of our congregation, standing on my doorstep with a bottle of root beer in one hand and a gallon of vanilla ice cream in the other. He raised the two items in the air slightly to ensure that I noticed them and then he announced:

"Some days you just need a root beer float."

"Great!" I said to myself. "Some church-going, do-gooder come to cheer me up and score a few points with the Man upstairs."

I wasn't going to drop my defenses or lay down my false front no matter what, but I invited him in, we prepared a couple of floats, then sat down at the kitchen table.

Marvin was an anomaly. He had an un-mistakeable aura of wealth around him, but his appearance was disheveled and unkempt. He looked like a sixties activist who had struck it rich in a capitalistic world but who couldn't fully forego his rebellious idealism and hippie hopefulness. Plus, he never wore socks. That might not be unusual for the sandal-clad beach goers, but Marvin wore pressed slacks and expensive Corthay shoes, just no socks. Ever.

As that first evening advanced, I downplayed my pain and built up my accomplishments. And Marvin simply listened. No judgment or accusation showed in his demeanor. His seemingly sincere interest in my welfare suggested nothing more than a compassionate soul who wanted to soothe my sorrows. It was hard not to pour my heart out to him. As the evening ended and I accompanied Marvin to the door, he casually remarked:

"We should do this again."

"Sure," I said, as I pushed the door closed and went back to my secure spot on the sofa.

The following Saturday, after the kids had been put to bed, there came a knock again, and there stood Marvin again, root beer and ice cream in hand. This became a pattern over the next several weeks.

Something about Marvin seemed to pull at the truth hidden inside me. He never asked; never pried, but somehow, I wanted to talk with him. I wanted to share my fears, my sorrows, my emptiness. And one evening I did. I opened my heart as tears welled up in my eyes.

"Don't you dare cry, you big sissy!" I shouted to myself.

But I cried anyway as I told Marvin of the fighting, the verbal and emotional abuse, the degrading and destructive language that had consumed and destroyed my family, my spirit, and, I was certain, even my salvation.

Marvin listened; un-accusing and non-judgmental in every way, offering only words of comfort where he could but mostly, simply hearing me pour my pain and sorrow like raw sewage into his warm and receptive soul.

With the kids being gone for the holidays and all the work I had done at the stables; I had completely forgotten that Marvin would be dropping by again this evening.

When Marvin asked if I was excited for Christmas, I confessed that I really didn't have the Christmas spirit this year. The kids would be back the day after Christmas and I'd celebrate with them, but for me, this Christmas was empty and shallow.

I didn't feel any love from Jesus. Academically, I understood that God loved me. In my head, I knew I could be forgiven, but in my heart, I felt nothing. I disclosed to Marvin that the chambers of my heart were so filled with worldly filth and carnal desires that the Spirit of God would never dare approach me. My depraved heart could never hold the purity of His love.

"Do you pray much?" Marvin asked.

"Pray?" I questioned. "No, not lately. I haven't really prayed in a while. I mean, I don't think God really cares to hear from a guy like me."

"You need to invite God back into your life, Mark, … back into your heart."

"Do you really think God wants to dwell in my heart?" I asked rather forcibly. "You ought to know better; God doesn't dwell in unholy temples, or something like that."

Marvin turned his gaze away from me looking instead at the little manger on the mantle across the room. My mother had left it to me, and I still followed her tradition of making it the centerpiece of my Christmas décor, even though one of the shepherd's crocks had broken off at the top and I was missing a wise man.

"What do you imagine Mary was thinking as she rode into Bethlehem, Mark?"

"What do you mean?" I asked.

"Look at your manger on the mantle. Do you think that's what Mary really hoped for? Do you think she rode into town, looked down the street at the stable and said: 'How quaint! That'll look so nice two thousand years from now displayed on everyone's mantle place. It'll be so pretty with a bit of Christmas garland around it, maybe some evergreen boughs on the side. I think I'll have my baby there.'"

"Well, if she did, she'd be pretty disappointed in mine. I don't even own any garland," I responded indifferently.

"Well, I don't think Mary wanted that at all. I think she longed for a comfortable bed to deliver her baby in. After seven days riding on a donkey, I think Mary wanted a room and a bed and a bath and probably a skilled mid-wife to lend her a hand."

"Well, we certainly don't always get what we want, do we?" I commented dryly.

"No, but this was the birth of the Only Begotten Son of God, the greatest birth of all time."

"Yeah," I remarked, "it was." And I believed that with all my heart.

"There is a reason why Jesus wasn't born in a sanitary hospital with clean sheets and skilled doctors and nurses in attendance with all the latest and greatest medical technology on hand. Because that's not what God wanted. Joseph Smith taught us that the Son of God descended below *all* things. Do you understand what that means, Mark?"

I confessed I did not, not fully anyway.

"I know you know what a stable is for, don't you?"

"Yeah. They keep the animals there."

"Exactly. So, imagine the number of travelers who must have arrived in Bethlehem that night. There was 'no room' at the inn, remember? And how did those travelers get there?"

"On foot. On donkeys, I guess. Probably on camels, too, I imagine."

"And while those weary travelers slept, all their animals had to be put up for the night somewhere, right?"

"Sure," I responded.

"So, where'd the inn keeper put them?"

"In the stable, of course." I started to wonder where Marvin was headed with all of this. He seemed to just be stating the obvious.

"Well, you have a stable, don't you, Mark?"

"Yeah. Yeah, I do."

"So, you know how messy they can be."

"Ugh," I grunted. "All too well, Marvin. You should have seen what I had to wade through today!"

"And you've just got the one horse," Marvin continued. "Imagine the filth of a stable filled with all the animals that had come to Bethlehem with their owners to be taxed and all housed in that tiny stable."

I sipped again at my root beer float.

"Look at Mary kneeling there, Mark.?"

I looked over again at the manger on the mantle.

"Do you think that's pristine hay she's knelling on, sent out every day to the local dry cleaners along with the bed sheets?"

"No."

"No, it isn't. Jesus was born in a disgusting, filthy stable where all those animals eat and sleep and defecate and … well, you know, … what I'm saying, Mark, is it wasn't just coincidence that there was no room at the inn. Jesus was born in a stable for a reason and it wasn't just so we could all have quaint Christmas decorations on our mantles. You see, Mark, Jesus has already experienced all the filth of this world. He was born right smack into the middle of it.

"What you hold in your heart," Marvin continued, "is no surprise to Him. He was born in muck and mire and manure and the most disgusting conditions you can imagine. The only way you're going to clean out your heart, Mark, is to invite Him in. He's been there already. He's not afraid of a little filth."

I gurgled the last sip of my root beer float, disrupting the spirit of our discussion. Marvin stood up to leave.

"Think about it, Mark. Your heart's no dirtier than your horse's stall or Mary's manger."

Before he left Marvin added: "And Mark, say a prayer tonight. Invite God back into your heart. Ask for His help."

"I'll think about it."

"No. I want you to promise me." Marvin reached out and took my arm. "Promise me, Mark."

"I don't know if that's a promise I can keep."

"Well, I'm not leaving until you do. Promise me you'll say a prayer tonight. Promise me you'll ask God to help you find your way."

I knew Marvin wouldn't go until I promised.

"Alright. I promise," I said, never really intending to keep it.

With that, Marvin closed the door and left.

Chapter Five

A Christmas Gift of Gratitude

It was late but I stayed up to do the dishes. Then I straightened up the kids' bedrooms and I laid out my best suit for Sunday services in the morning. Finally, I sat down on the sofa and flipped the T.V. back on. The sofa had become my bed since the divorce. Sleeping in the bedroom was simply too painful. In fact, the only way I *could* sleep without sedatives was, as my favorite poet, Leonard Cohen, had said, by 'getting lost in that hopeless little screen.' Without the distraction of the television set, my mind just kept dredging up my sordid past.

A re-run of *M*A*S*H,* which I'd probably seen a dozen times, was airing and I settled in for what I hoped would be a solid night's sleep. I drifted in and out of slumber, being roused mostly by the loud late-night commercials, but as I pressed the off button on the remote to finally call it a night, my mind returned from its dreamy recesses.

"You promised Marvin," it scolded me.

"I know, but I'm too tired and you know we're never going to get an answer anyway," I responded.

"You promised," came the unsolicited reply.

Almost angrily and certainly annoyed, I threw off my blanket and got down on my knees.

I have prayed ever since I was a child and yet, I was never certain if God was listening and I wondered if He ever answered. If I was sick and my parents prayed for me, I recovered. But other kids whose parents didn't even believe in God got sick and recovered without the benefit of prayer. If I lost something and prayed to find it, sometimes I did and sometimes I didn't, as did the kids who didn't pray. I wanted to believe in the power of prayer. I wanted to know that God was listening, but even as I got down on my knees beside my sofa, I knew that God wouldn't answer me. In that moment, I couldn't really think of a specific time when He ever had.

"Fine," I told myself. "I promised I'd do it, so I'll do it."

I knew it would be a wasted effort, but I could quickly ask God to help me and then just jump back on my couch and finally go to sleep.

"Heavenly Father," I mumbled.

No, I'll be honest, it was more of a grumble. I didn't believe tonight's prayer would change anything. It simply wouldn't make any difference but suddenly, as the words escaped my lips, something did change. Something changed in me.

I suddenly felt strangely grateful, something I had not felt in years. I had often heard the expression, 'my heart swelled within me,' but I had never felt it; not until tonight anyway. I began to voice my gratitude in a sincere outpouring to my Father in Heaven.

"Thank you for my two beautiful children," I began and with each expression came another thought, another blessing in my pitiful life that I had forgotten about or dismissed. Blessing after blessing flowed unsolicited into my mind and gratitude poured from my wounded heart as unabated tears coursed down my cheeks.

A full fifteen minutes must have gone by before my mind began to slow down and I started to feel that I had 'covered' every good thing in my life. I know that to some, fifteen minutes may not seem like much, but to those of us who were more the thanks-for-everything-and-bless-'em-all type, fifteen minutes was almost an eternity.

Now, all that remained was for me to ask God for His help. I longed for an answer. Or maybe I didn't. Maybe I was afraid of the answer that would be waiting for someone like me. Maybe I'd be better off not hearing from the Pure and Holy Being whose anger and offense I had surely incurred.

The Heavens had seemed closed to me for so long that

even now, even with my unsolicited outpouring of gratitude, I did not really expect God to answer me.

"Father," I continued timidly…

Chapter Six

Feel His Words

When Nephi, a Book of Mormon prophet, was commanded by God to build a ship to carry him and his family across the seas to the Promised Land, Nephi's brothers, Laman and Lemuel, rebelled and refused to work. Nephi called them to repentance (once again) and reminded them that they had seen an angel of the Lord.

Inscribing this event on to the Plates of Nephi, the young prophet makes a revelatory and insightful observation recorded in 1st Nephi, chapter 17, verse 45.

"Ye have seen an angel," he reminds his brothers, "and he spake unto you; yea, ye have heard his voice from time to time; and he hath spoken to you in a still, small voice."

Nothing out of the ordinary there, except, you know, the fact that they actually saw and heard an angel, but otherwise, pretty standard scriptural stuff. The next line, however, is a little distinct and much more perceptive.

"… but ye were past feeling," Nephi points out to them, "that ye could not *feel* his words."

Isn't it interesting that Nephi doesn't say, "ye were past hearing that ye could not hear his words" but instead uses the descriptive term, "feeling?" Could it be that when angels speak to us, when spiritual voices whisper, we don't so much hear their words as feel them in our hearts?

I don't know if this is the way it works in every case, but apparently, this was the experience Laman and Lemuel had. It was also the experience I was about to have kneeling by my couch wondering if God was listening, questioning if He even heard the petitions of my sinful heart.

"Father," I pleaded. "I need Your help."

The very moment I uttered these words the voice of the Lord entered my heart. It wasn't a voice I heard. It was actually more tangible than that; it was a voice I felt. The words of the Lord, real, physical, as tangible as any solid object I ever held in my hand, entered my heart. I felt actual words.

Christ didn't condemn me to hell, thank Goodness; nor did He say, 'My son, your sins are forgiven. Go in peace.' His words were more pertinent, more needed and appropriate for me; and infinitely comforting in their context.

He kindly and lovingly answered:

"I'm so glad you finally came to me with your problems."

My life didn't change overnight. In fact, it got worse before it got better. But no matter how bad the days and the nights became, no matter how far I strayed and wandered and then wandered back and strayed again, I now knew and understood and felt, yes, mostly I felt, deep within my heart, that I was not alone in this wicked world; that no matter how far I had trudged into the filth and the muck and the mire of errant living, there is always a hand extended, a voice constantly calling, a Savior silently listening. The once-baby King, born in the muck and mire of a filthy stable, waits patiently for us to welcome Him into the darkest recesses of our own sinful hearts.

Jesus Christ is the only One who can clean out our stables because He is the only One who descended below all things so that He *could* be invited into our lowly and loathsome lives.

I have told this story as honestly as I could, in the hope that it reaches someone, anyone, who feels they cannot be forgiven, that God would turn away from them because of the sins that weigh on their hearts, that they have strayed too far from His reach. If, by chance, you are that person, I invite you to make yourself a root beer float and think about the Baby in the manger, the manger on the mantle, and promise me, (because I'm not leaving until you do,) that you will welcome the Savior back into your life.

Don't determine to make your heart a hospitable and

sociable environment first. Don't attempt to clean up the mess on your own. You can't. Not alone. You, like all of us, need the help and strength of our loving Savior, Jesus Christ. Let Him experience the mire that you have been wallowing in for so long now. Let Him clean out your stable.

"Come now, and let us reason together, saith the Lord: though your sins be as scarlet, they shall be as white as snow; though they be red like crimson, they shall be as wool."

Isaiah 1:18

I hope you enjoyed this little book and that it helped you to sense the love and compassion that your Savior feels for you.

I would love it if you could post an honest 5-star review on Amazon or some other book site where you have an account and posting privileges. Maybe you can mention what you liked best about it or how it helped you in some way.

If you found this book enjoyable or inspirational, I would hope that you tell your friends about it.

About the Author

Bill Wylson is the author of over 50 published writings dealing with family values, religious issues and religious education. His work has appeared in The Ensign, This People, Liberty Magazine, Success, and others.

Bill graduated from the Columbia School of Broadcasting in Hollywood, CA as a commercial copywriter. He wrote trade journal ads for a major advertising agency in Los Angeles and public service announcements for a Los Angeles television station. He also wrote and produced corporate video presentations.

He has served as a volunteer Board Member of Advocates of Single Parent Youth, Special Fun Games for the Disabled, and on the Boards of Arts and Theater Councils. He has also served on Advisory Committees for the Volunteer Center of Los Angeles and on the United Way Government Affairs Committee.

Bill Wylson currently lives with his wife, Connie, in Salt Lake City, Utah.

Other Books by Bill Wylson:

Hieroglyphs, Golden Plates and Typos:
How "Corrections" in the Book of Mormon Prove Its Authenticity.

On the inside cover of his first leather-bound Book of Mormon my father had written the following quotation from the prophet Joseph Smith: "I told the brethren that the Book of Mormon was the most correct of any book on earth, and the keystone of our religion, and a man would get nearer to God by abiding by its precepts, than by any other book." Directly below this quote, my father had compiled a list of scriptures which he had labeled: *"Mistakes in the Book of Mormon."*

Committing his writings to the future reader, Moroni candidly and apologetically acknowledged: "And if there be faults they be the faults of a man. But behold, we know no fault."

How then did my father have the boldness to make a list of mistakes in the Book of Mormon? To gain a better understanding of these 'corrections' in the Book of Mormon and how they testify to its truthfulness and authenticity, we need to understand the process involved in making plates of ore and the method for inscribing on them.

Elder Hammond and the Inspector

"You know, there's a word to describe someone who won't even bother to meet his new companion at the bus station. It starts with an 'O' or, I don't know, maybe a 'C' or something. I think it's C-a—. No, I've lost it."

Elder Hammond was a freckled-face, shy sort of bumpkin from some rural farm town in Kansas. He was awkward and withdrawn. Even in his white shirt and tie he reminded you of the type of kid you'd see in denim coveralls, wearin' a straw hat and chompin' on a thin blade of grass whilst irrigatin' the lower forty.

I actually knew nothing about Elder Hammond's personal life. He was just a simple, quiet, humble boy but he was also determined and dedicated. He had no delusions of grandeur, just a desire to serve. Perhaps more than any missionary I had ever met, Elder Hammond had a purity of spirit and an altruistic motivation in ministering. I pitied him. I think he actually believed he could make a difference.

Three Minutes Eighteen Seconds:
A Prophet's Final Message to the World

Words are extremely powerful. Lord Byron poetically portrays this truth:

"But words are things, and a small drop of ink,
Falling like dew, upon a thought, produces
That which makes thousands, perhaps millions, think."

Three Minutes Eighteen Seconds examines three "small drops of ink" that are, simultaneously, extremely powerful words spoken by President Thomas S. Monson in the April 2017 General Conference.

Give Place in Your Heart:
31 Promises from the Book of Mormon

All of us are familiar with Moroni's promise that Christ will manifest the truth of the Book of Mormon to us by the power of the Holy Ghost. This is just one of many promises the Lord has made regarding the Book of Mormon. In *Give Place in Your Heart,* Bill Wylson outlines 31 promises, with their attendant blessings and conditions, that the Lord would love to bestow upon you.

www.ingramcontent.com/pod-product-compliance
Lightning Source LLC
LaVergne TN
LVHW012340100826
845148LV00018B/3215